AI
& CHESS

ARYA SHAH

ISBN: 978-1-9162173-8-6 (Ebook)

978-1-9162173-9-3 (Paperback)

Email: aryarsh33@gmail.com

Published by PaperTrue, in the United States of America.

First edition 2020.

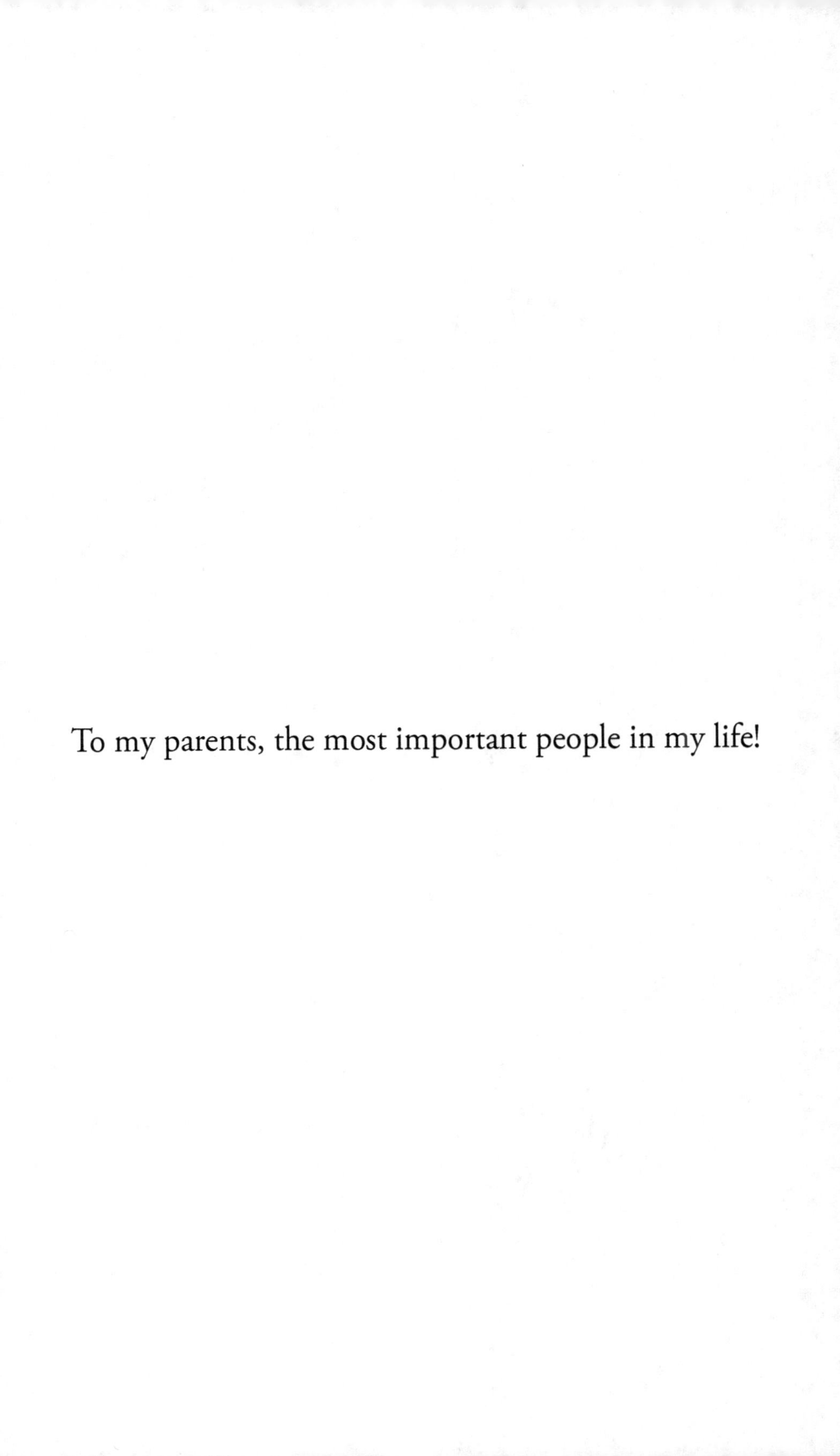

To my parents, the most important people in my life!

AI
&CHESS

Special Thanks

To all my teachers at Overseas Family School, I would also like to thank the Singapore Chess Federation for helping me pursue my Chess Career!

Thank you!

AI

&CHESS

Contents

AI

&CHESS

Foreword

Chess as a game has been undergoing lot of changes over the decades. As the game is evolving with the help of strong players introducing new ways of approaching a position on one side, the influence of technology on chess, has been even more impactful in multiple ways.

Initially, computers helped mainly as a storing platform. We can store vast data in small space and also access it with the help of software like Chessbase. Subsequently, powerful analytical engines were introduced which could analyse complex positions in matter of seconds and give a better assessment of the position.

With advances being made in both software and hardware, we reached appoint where the engines could defeat even a World Champion without too much effort. Just when it looked like the role of technology has reached its peak out came the Artificial Intelligence and Machine learning.

In this book, young and talented Arya has captured the role and evolution of AI in simple terms which is easy to absorb and assimilate. I learnt many useful information regarding and now feel more knowledgeable than before reading this book.

I strongly recommend this book to anyone who is interested to know the direction Chess will progress in the future.

GM RB Ramesh
Indian National Chess Coach

AI
&CHESS

Introduction

The first part of this book will cover how chess engines have affected chess players in the long run. The second part of this book will discuss various ways in which this technology will impact the future generations of chess players and also expand on how chess, on the whole, has been impacted—from the time of Kasparov to the time of AlphaGo Zero and the future.

Enjoy reading!!

AI
&CHESS

Chapter 1

What is Artificial Intelligence?

Before we begin evaluating chess engines and how artificial intelligence (AI) impacts chess, let's first understand the basic concepts. AI is an area of computer science which helps in the creation of machines which "work and relate like a human" (Artificial Intelligence, Technopia). This could be termed as human intelligence. In short, AI is defined as human intelligence inputted in machines. AI is designed to carry out a few activities such as

- Speech Recognition, Voice Recognition

- Machine Learning

- Reasoning

In this chapter, each of these characteristics will be thoroughly explained.

Speech Recognition

What is speech and voice recognition?

Speech and voice recognition are a form of AI. Voice Recognition is to identify an individual voice, whereas speech recognition relates to identifying spoken words and translating them to make correct sense. (All you need to know about voice recognition, Bhagat, Bajaj)

History of speech and voice recognition

1950s–1965

- Voice recognition dates to the early 1950s. The first speech recognition system was designed by Bell Laboratories which could identify words but not numbers. This was known as the Audrey system which could recognize a single voice speaking digits aloud.

- In 1962, IBM introduced shoebox which understood and responded to 16 words in English. 1970s

- Carnegie Mellon's "Harpy" speech system came from this program and was capable of understanding over 1,000. This was done with the help of the US Department of Defence and DARPA.

- Bell Laboratories introduced a system which could interpret multiple voices just like Siri. 1980s

- The hidden Markov method was one of the significant breakthroughs in 1980s. Until then, most software were just using words and sound patterns. Using the hidden Markov estimated the probability of unknown sounds that could be words.

1990s

- Due to the invention of personal computers and faster processors, it was easier to use software; for example, Dragon Dictate was used.

2000s

- Speech recognition had almost achieved full perfection, which was up to 80% according to PC World. For almost a decade, there were not many advancements, until in November 2008, when tech giant Google came up with the voice search. Providing voice search as an app made it accessible for many millions of people. Today, we can see speech recognition being used everywhere. Below is an image which shows how speech recognition has taken place in our modern world.

How does it work?

Though there are various intricate steps involved, speech and voice recognition both work on the same principle. When you speak, you create vibrations in the air. The computer takes this vibration as analog data and converts this it into digital data. The analog-to-digital converter (ADC) executes this for the computer. The ADC samples the sound by taking precise measurements of the wave at frequent intervals. The computer would then discard the unwanted noise. It uses different bands of frequency to separate these noises. This signal is divided at a range from a few hundredths a second to sometimes a few thousand a second. The range will go this high if the sound is a plosive sound constant. Plosive constant sounds are sounds which are caused when the airflow is barricaded.

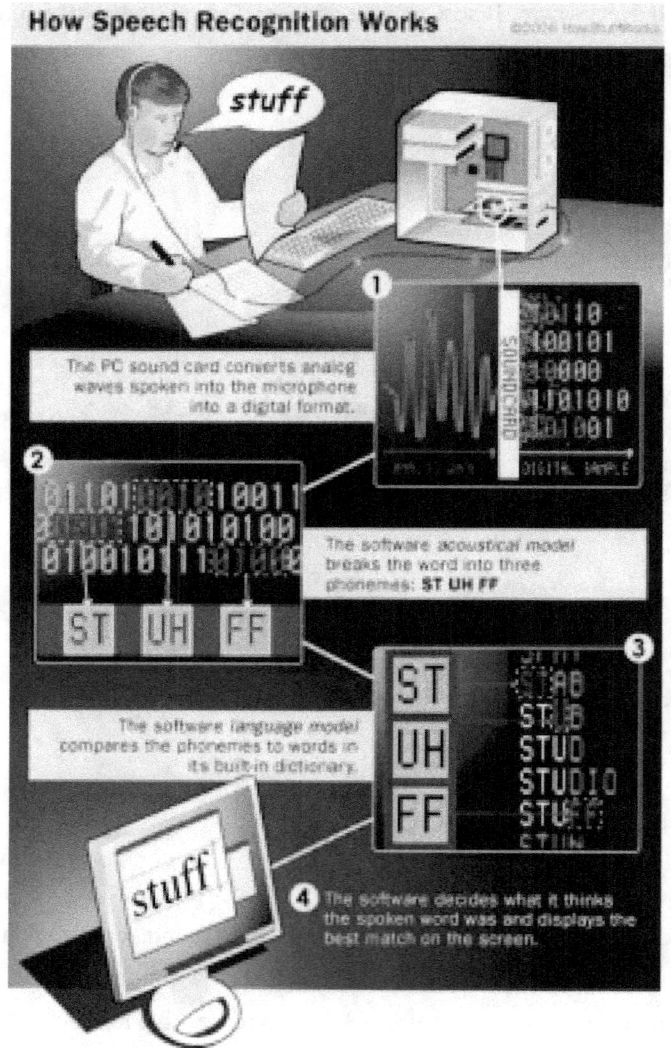

Where do you use it in everyday life?

Today, we use speech and voice recognition for many things—from Siri to speech typing and Google Home and Alexa and other such devices. Siri answers our day-to-day questions but Google Home and Amazon's Alexa take speech and voice recognition to a different level. Google Home can turn on and switch off lights in your house, conduct Google searches and much more. We will investigate what comes after AI in the next chapter.

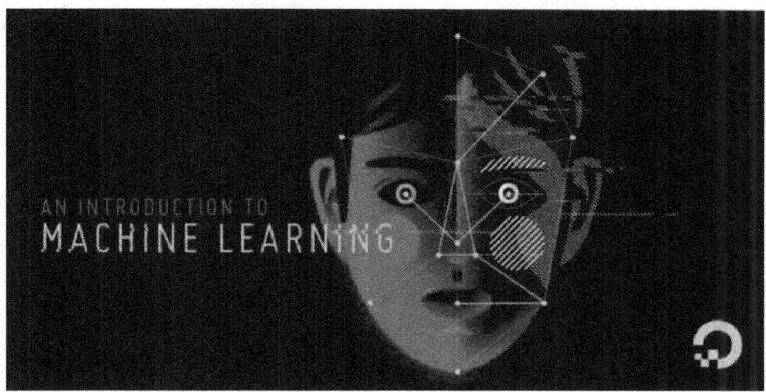

Machine learning

Machine learning is a very important subset of AI. Machine learning focuses on the development of computer programs that can access and learn data. The aim of this is to make the machines learn by themselves. Data is the manner in which machines can learn by themselves. Machine learning will be one of the key subsets of AI we will be discussing in the later chapters. The Cambridge Dictionary defines data as information, especially facts or numbers, collected to be examined and considered and used to help decision-making, or information in an electronic form that can be stored and used by a computer.

This same data helps the computer learn, as the documentary "The AI Race" states, data is the new oil!

History of Machine Learning

1950s

– In 1950, Alan Turning created the Turning Test to determine if computers had real intelligence; to pass the test, the computer had to fool the actual human being by telling him that it is also human.

– In 1952, IBM wrote the first computer learning program. The program was written for the game of checkers. The computer would play this game by itself and improved and came up with chess strategies.

- In 1957, Frank Roosevelt came up with the first neural network for the computer which could restore the human brain.

1960s

- In 1967, the computers were able to recognize basic patterns with the help of the algorithm of the nearest neighbors. The nearest neighbor could be used in finding the route for a journey.

1970s

- At Stanford, students created a cart which could navigate obstacles in a room on its own. This dealt more with the ability to move objects but it also comes under machine learning.

1980s

- Explanation Based Learning (EBL) was introduced in 1981where the computer could come up with its own general rule; other than that, everything else was discarded.

1990s

- The data story finally starts. Computer scientists start creating machines which would use data to come up with a conclusion.

- IBM's Deep Blue defeats Garry Kasparov. 2000s

- The term deep learning was coined in 2006 by Geoffrey Hinton.

2010s

- Microsoft released Kinect which could relate to human features which allowed people to interact with machines using human features.

- In 2011, IBM's Watson beat humans at "Jeopardy!"

- Google Brain with the neural network can identify an object.

- Google develops a machine learning algorithm which can detect cats in YouTube videos.

- A machine learning platform is developed by Amazon

- In 2016, AlphaGo beats the best Go player in the world. This was developed by Google.

- In 2017, AlphaZero, a computer program which was developed Alphabet's subsidiary DeepMind, beats Stockfish 9 in chess by just learning chess in 4 hours. Vidit Gujrathi, India's super grandmaster, terms AlphaGo Zero as alien.

- In 2018, IBM's Watson develops a machine learning algorithm which can debate with humans.

Where do we use machine learning now?

- GPS systems like Google Maps, using machine learning, can predict the possibility of traffic or congestion in an area.

- Search engine results are based on machine learning technologies

- As of now, machine learning is used by very few people who have access to Wi-Fi, but it is expected to be used in self-driving cars, chess engines like AlphaGo Zero and others.

Reasoning

Reasoning is when AI can generate a conclusion from the available knowledge; AI is able to do this using logical techniques using deduction. Chess engines like Fritz and Stockfish also use techniques of deduction by creating their own knowledge but not from the available knowledge. Reasoning is a coming boom which has been deployed by many tech giants like Google, Amazon and Netflix. We will investigate reasoning in the second part.

AI
&CHESS

Chapter 2

What Does AI Have to Do with Chess?

What does AI have to do with chess? This is exactly the question this chapter is going to answer!

Whenever someone says anything related to Technology and chess The first thing that would come to your mind would be chess engines, and when I ask you the question: What does AI have to do with Chess? Well you probably would say "Something related to Chess Engines.." Well you are absolutely right! During the last few years, Artificial Intelligence has made a significant impact on the Chess World -- All thanks to Deepmind; a UK based company found in 2010, acquired by Google in 2014. How is Deepmind transforming Chess by the use of AI? Before knowing about how Deepmind is transforming Chess we have to first know about what Deepmind did with Go in 2016! For those who don't really know what Go is here is a Wikipedia(Don't worry it's accurate) definition-- *"Go is an abstract strategy board game for two players, in which the aim is to surround more territory than the opponent. The game was invented in China more than 2,500 years ago and is believed to be the oldest board game continuously played to the present day."* Go is also played on different grids-- For example: 19 x 19, 13 x 13, and 9 x 9. Usually the bigger the Grid size the harder it is to play against the computer. Coming back to Artificial Intelligence and Go, Go was always considered to be a very hard challenge in Artificial Intelligence and it is also much more difficult than Chess to program it on a computer. Here are quotes from Mathematician I. J good to understand how difficult Go is: *"Go on a computer? – In order to programme a computer to play a reasonable game of Go, rather than merely a legal game – it is necessary to formalise the principles of good strategy, or to design a learning programme. The principles are more qualitative and mysterious than in chess, and depend more on judgment. So I think it will be even more difficult to programme a computer to play a reasonable game of Go than of chess."* Here is just a brief idea of how complicated go is: Go has an estimated 10^{171} possible variations that could be played! The estimated amount of atoms in the world are about 10^{81}!!

Before Alpha Go even came into the picture, Go programs were barely able to beat Amatuer go players that too on a 9 x 9 board. Then came AlphaGo, which took the Go World by Storm, just take a look at AlphaGo's accomplishments:

- October 2015: AlphaGo beat's Fan Hui, the european Go Champion (Before this Go Programs could barely beat amateur players)

- March 2016: AlphaGo beat's Lee Sedol(Professional Go player) 4-1.

- May 2017: AlphaGo beat's Ke Jie who was ranked number one in the world during that time.

- October 2017 AlphaGoZero is released which surpasses its previous versions, beating AlphaGo(previous version which did beat the best Go players) 100 games to 0.

NOTE: Before AlphaGo came into the picture Go Programs could barely beat **amateurs** on a 9 x 9 grid.

This technology was later replicated by Deepmind, where alphaZero learns chess(instead of go) on its own and beats the best chess engine in the world--Stockfish.

You can find games played by Alpha Go Zero in the Appendix, YouTube Videos are also provided which analyse these games.

Leela Chess engine is another chess engine that we can associate with Artificial Intelligence, Leela is a free open source neural network based chess engine whose methods are based on the AlphaGo Zero and the Alpha Zero Project.

Chapter 3

History of Computer Chess

Chess has been a very popular sport for over 600 years. In fact, the first recorded game in the chess mega database was played in 1419, as shown in Figure 2.

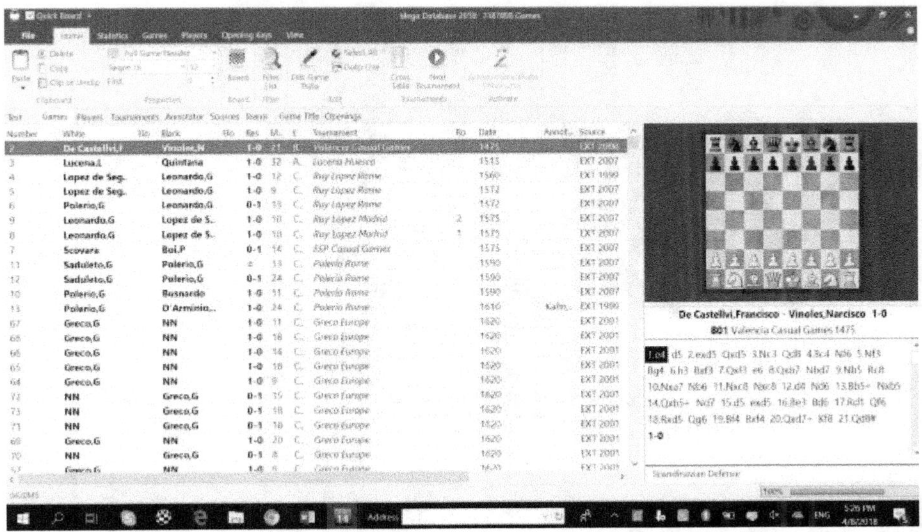

As you can see, the first game was played in 1475. As rich is the sport's history so is the number of people play it. According to a study conducted by AGON, there are "approximately the same number of chess players as regular Facebook members, and in the U.S., more people play chess than tennis and golf, combined!" Chess first originated in India in the 6th century BC. Until the 19th century, chess was not played officially until Wilhelm Steinitz became the first world champion. Even then, it wasn't that prominent a game, as when he was crowed the world champion, his prize winning was only 800 euros, whereas today, the net worth of the top chess player is about 10 million US dollars with earnings of about 2 million US dollars a month. It would be impossible to cover all the minor details about the history of chess; hence, we will just focus on the history of computer chess.

History of Computer Chess

The first computer chess was created in the year 1770 when Wolfgang Von Kempelen invented the Turk to impress Maria Thresa of Austria. The Turk was a chess playing machine which was used to beat human opponents. The base cabinet could be opened to reveal a complex mechanism, but the mechanism was a disguise—a human chess player could squeeze behind it and control the moves of the automaton.

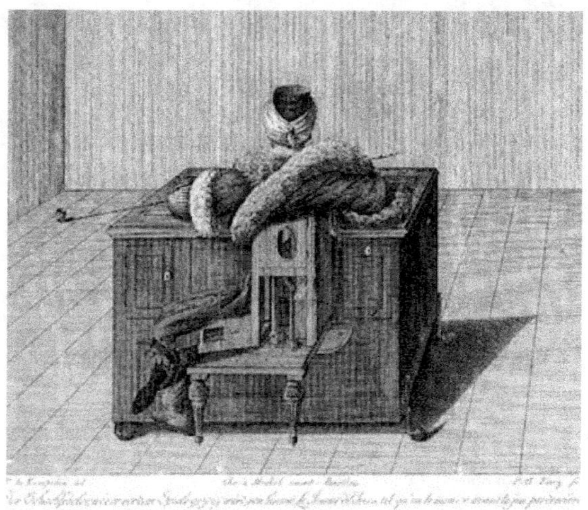

The hoax was revealed almost 100 years after it was built. Figure 3 shows the image of the Turk. We will not go into much detail about the Turk, but due to the Turk, humans began to start working on chess engines. In 1951, the investigation of chess playing computers started. Turning began investigating chess playing computers with a paper and pencil where he himself played the role of the machine Later in the same year, his colleague Dietrich Prinz wrote the first chess playing program. The program created by Prinz was not able to play the whole game during that time because of processor, hardware and memory problems though it could successfully solve mate in two moves. Figure 4 is an example of a mate in two moves which the computer could have solved; see if you can solve it.

In 1958, Alex Bernstein wrote the first chess program which could play a complete chess game. The program worked on IBM 704, IBM's mainframe computer. Figure 5 illustrates this humongous computer.

This computer may be gigantic, but the hardware power of this computer would be less than any of our normal personal computers or maybe even some of the current smartphones. In 1962, a chess program designed by MIT students could beat amateur chess players. In 1967, Richard Greenblatt incorporated many powerful heuristics to the chess program of 1962. Heuristics is nothing but the ability to solve problems. Figure 6 demonstrates a clear image of what a heuristic is.

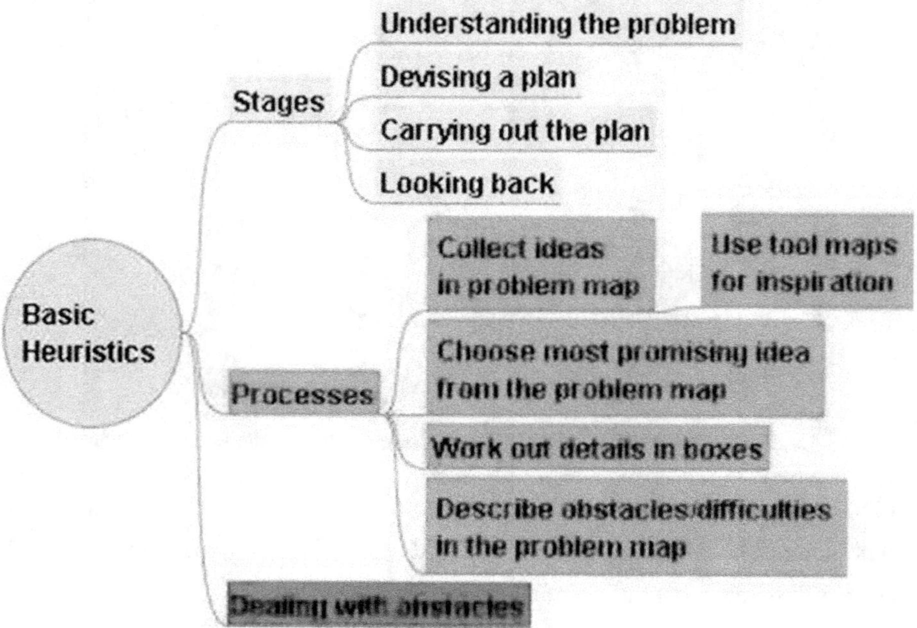

In 1970s, chess playing software were just improving because of improved hardware and better processor speed. More and more effective heuristics were added. Chess playing computers had achieved the strength of FIDE Elo of 1400 of today. By the late 1970s, computer chess began threating master level chess. In 1968, international master David Levy bet researcher John McClarty that no chess engine could beat him in 10 years. This bet was taken seriously, and a chess game between a chess engine and Mr.

Levy was played. Any guesses for the result? Well, international master Levy won, beating the chess program. The era of personal computers had come by, making chess engines more and more stronger.

In 1980, for the first time, there was a competition for just chess playing computers and there was also an award of $100000 for anyone who would beat Anatoly Karpov, the world chess champion during that time. In 1988, Deep Thought was invented, which could beat grandmasters; it was a big milestone crossed in grandmaster chess. Deep Thought then played Garry Kasparov, the then world champion. Deep Thought lost two exhibition games against Kasparov. Soon after this IBM, purchased Deep Thought and created a special group of researchers to improve the chess program with the aim to beat Garry Kasparov.

A rematch was held again in 1997. To understand this better, we will be looking at the first game played by Kasparov and Deep Blue with the help of my annotations

(1) Kasparov, Garry (2785) - Comp Deep Blue [A07] New York Man-Machine New York (1), 03.05.1997 [AryArsh]

1.Nf3 d5 2.g3 Bg4 3.b3

[Kasparov plays a very quiet opening—not a bad idea against a computer. The main reason for this is because it will be able to take the computer out of the opening preparation and its books, thereby leaving it clueless and could take up more time.]

3...Nd7 4.Bb2 e6 5.Bg2 Ngf6 6.0–0 c6 7.d3 Bd6 8.Nbd2 0–0 9.h3 Bh5

[We have reached a position which has occurred many times in master and grandmaster chess. White's basic plan is to gain space in the center with e4. Black will sooner or later have to deal with the threat of e5, either by moving his pieces or by playing e5. Later, there will be a slight weakness on f5 which would be exploited by Nh4–f5. Now, this maneuver is impossible because the f3–knight is pinned. This is sometimes the reason why white plays qe1.]

10. e3 [A very unusual move. There were no examples of this before this game was played. The normal moves here are 10 e4 and 10 Qe1. Of the two, I would judge 10 e4 to be the more flexible. In this way, White can reserve the option of either Qe1 or Qe2, depending on Black's reply. The advantages of e3 are hard to find; Kasparov soon adopts the Qe1 and e4 plan but havs lost a tempo in the process. Perhaps his idea was simply to take Deep Blue out of its opening book which, as mentioned earlier, could be a very nice strategy against a chess engine.]

10...h6 [[#]]

Kasparov's move now looks good. Instead of putting the extra tempo to use by developing queenside counter play, for example by playing a5, the computer makes a pawn move which is worse than useless, because it weakens the kingside slightly. In a few moves, we will see the importance of this. Now that the extra tempo has been handed back, the balance again slightly favors White and now it feels like the computer does not have any idea of what is going on.]

11. Qe1 Qa5 [Deep Blue's play is weird and is not quite clear. Ba3 to exchange the active bishop on b2 could be a plan, but this plan is easily countered, and then the queen is doing nothing on a5.]

12. a3 Bc7?! [And this is very odd. There are two possible reasons behind this move. First, it may simply be anticipating e4–e5 by White; secondly, Deep Blue may want to have its queen defended in case of a line such as]

12...Rad8 13.Bxf6 Nxf6 14.Ne4 Qxe1 15.Nxf6+ gxf6 16.Rfxe1 [Although this is nothing to fear as Black's active bishops easily compensate for the insignificant, but it would weaken the kingside; I would prefer 12...Bg6 which prepares to answer e4 by ...e5. The prophylactic Bg6 is necessary in this case because e5 can be met by Nh4. This is particularly strong because of the waste of tempo Deep Blue did with h6, which means that after a possible exchange of knight for bishop on g6, Black cannot make the natural recapture with the h-pawn. Thus, Black must play ...Bg6 in advance, ready to meet Nh4 by ...Bh7. In this phase of the game, Deep Blue just responds to each problem on a move-by-move, without creating any plan for developing counter play. In this respect, Kasparov's choice of opening appears very intelligent. We can now clearly see that there are many advantages of taking the computer out of the opening play. It does not have any clear plan, nor it has any way to intercept what is going on. The computer is clueless. If the same position was played today, it could be different as the chess engines easily know what to do.]

13. Nh4 [An awkward move for the computer. The move could also look weird to a club player but the maneuver of the knight to f5 is a good plan. The threat is 14 g4 Bg6 Nxg6, and Black must make the ugly capture fxg6. I think that this would have been a lesser evil for Black, but White is still better because of the very ugly pawn structure.]

13...g5?

[This further weakens the f5 square, but White cannot do anything for now. After the pawn lever e4, the weakened f5 square would be clearly visible.]

14. Nhf3 e5 [All this looks horrible to the human eye. Having pushed both e- and g- pawns, the f5 square has become a big weakness. If White could plant a knight there, then the game would be completely won for White. Of course, Deep Blue is not very stupid. There is no straightforward route by which a knight can reach

the key square. Even then this long-term weakness remains a lasting burden for Black. White could potentially have great control over the white squares. Even then, there are no white pieces to exploit the weakened light squares. A weakness is not a weakness until not exploited.]

15. e4 [Kasparov tries to gain as much control as possible on the f5 square. This move still has a few drawbacks; it makes the bishop on g2 passive. This is not permanent unless the horrible move d4 is played.]

15...Rfe8 [15...d4 16.Qc1 Qa6 17.a4 c5 18.Kh2 Qe6 19.Nc4 Ne8 20.h4 gxh4 (20...g4 21.Nfd2 This is the variation recommended by Deep Fritz 13. Even though the bishop on g2 is blocked, the knights are jumping here and there. If Black tries to open the position with f5, then the bishop on g2 could potentially be a deadly beast.)]

16. Nh2 [Kasparov is careful. His plan is Qc1, Re1 and then Nf1–e3–f5. This is rather slow, but as White's position is solid, it is hard to come up with a plan for Black.]

[So far as I can see, he could have started this plan immediately with 16.Qc1, since 16...g4 is not a worry because of 17.Nh4 and the knight takes a short cut to f5.]

16...Qb6

[Still Deep Blue has a solid position but is without a plan.]

17. Qc1 a5 [At last Deep Blue hits upon a plan for developing counter play, although in this position, it is not very effective. The natural follow-up is ...a4 to restrict b4, and then c5. However, c5 is hard to arrange because of the pressure on d5, and if Black exchanges first on e4, then the route Nc4–e3–f5 is opened for the knight on d2. We can see how, time and time again, Black's natural plans are not effective because they would seriously expose the weakness on f5.]

18. Re1 Bd6 19.Ndf1 dxe4 [Now that the knight has moved away from d2, the possibility of Nc4 disappears and so this exchange becomes feasible. However, the knight is already on its way to f5 by a different route.]

20.dxe4 [20.Bxe4!? Nxe4 21.dxe4 This was an interesting way to get rid of the bad bishop but this, at the same time, leaves many light square weakness, and at the same time, Black has a bishop pair which could be dangerous in the endgame. For now, even though knights are better, the position could be quite be easily opened with f5 in the future. I think that the position is quite unbalanced but surely Deep Fritz prefers Black's position because of the bishop pair.]

20...Bc5 21.Ne3 [Trying to get it to f5.]

21...Rad8 22.Nhf1 [Black has hit upon a good method of keeping the knight out of f5, but just for now. The f2 pawn is quite hard to defend, and until White softens the pressure against it along the b6–f2 diagonal, the knight cannot go to f5. Kasparov's idea also could be to go to c4 via d2. If Black wants to maintain the pressure against f2, he must play ...Qa7, but White continues with b4, exploiting the line-up of a1–rook with the enemy queen, and Black is in trouble. The position is surely unclear.]

22...g4 [The computer tries to disturb White's plan. Although this move creates further kingside weaknesses, it enables Black to develop some piece activity. This is the critical phase. Everybody who has played a computer knows the scenario— you get a winning position; the computer makes some desperate tactical jump; you make a couple of inaccuracies and suddenly, the machine is all over you and you may even be losing.]

23.hxg4 Nxg4 24.f3? [In this desire to achieve his strategic need, Kasparov commits an inaccuracy which allows the machine to develop significant counter play. Kasparov just wanted all the advantage but this is not possible.]

[The most obvious plan is 24.Nxg4 Bxg4 25.Ne3. Kasparov probably realized that after 25...Be6. It is not so easy to make progress, because Black has maneuvered his light-squared bishop to a reasonable active square. For example, 26 Qd1, heading for h5, is met by 26...Bd4. However, I think that this was his best option; after 26.Re2 Kh7 27.Qe1, White's remaining pieces come into play, and Black's kingside weaknesses are not going to run away. Here, for example, 27...Bd4 runs into kommt 28.Bxd4 exd4 29.Nd5! cxd5 30.exd5 with a huge advantage for White.]

24...Nxe3 25.Nxe3 Be7!

[A very nice move. A human would find it hard to give away the pressure on the b6–g1 diagonal, but the computer spots that the bishop has an even better square on g5, both shielding the kingside weaknesses and pinning the e3–knight from a different place.]

26.Kh1 Bg5 27.Re2 [Kasparov recovers well. He intends Qg1 followed by Nf5, and the damage is repaired, but the computer strikes first.]

27...a4 [A good move. As we shall see, now the c4 is all for Black and a few holes in White's pawn structures. White cannot really take on a4 as the pawn structure is terrible, and Black has more than enough compensation.]

28. b4 f5 [Correct. Black must make use of his temporary piece activity to counter play. Passive play would allow White to get back on track and will give Kasparov his strategic needs.]

29. exf5!? [If White tries 29.Qe1 fxe4 30.Nc4 Qa6, now we see why one reason why Black prepared this line with a4. The attack against the c4–knight is awkward. 31.Rxe4 Nf6 and White must give some material. He will always get some compensation, for example, here, Nxe5 is unclear, but at least Deep Blue has made the game unclear from a much worse position. The move Kasparov plays also involves an exchange sacrifice.]

29...e4 30.f4 Bxe2 [30...Bxf4 31.gxf4 Bxe2 32.Qd2 Bh5 forced, or else White has the possibility of Ng4 33.Qc3 Re7 34.Nc4 Qc7 35.Qh8+ Kf7 36.Qxh6 and wins.]

31. fxg5 Ne5 [Black must block the long diagonal.] [31...hxg5 32.Nd5 wins at once.]

32. g6 [32.gxh6 Kh7 is a more reasonable reply, when Black has much better chances. (32...Rd6? 33.Nc4!)]

32...Bf3 33.Bc3 [A good prophylactic move. In many lines, the queens are exchanged, or White would like to send his queen away to the kingside. In these cases, it is important not to allow ...Rd2.]

33...Qb5? [A serious error. Deep Blue sees that this will probably lead to the exchange of queens and has no Black material advantage. However, in the end, White's advanced pawns and general grip on the position count for more than the small material addition of rook for bishop and pawn. Instead, Black should have kept the queens on the board.]

[33...h5 is one possibility. In many lines, Black gains a tempo because White cannot now play his queen to f1 in one move. One line runs 34.Qe1 Qb5 35.Qf1 Ng4 36.Nxg4 (36.Qxb5 cxb5 37.f6 Nxe3 38.f7+ Kf8 39.fxe8Q+ Rxe8 40.Bxf3 exf3 41.Kg1 is probably a draw) 36...hxg4 37.Qxb5 cxb5 38.f6 Re6 and Black can defend. Another idea is 33...Qc7. The queen goes to the kingside.]

34. Qf1 Qxf1+ [Now 34...Ng4 is impossible because of unmöglich wegen 35.Qxb5 cxb5 36.Nxg4 Bxg4 37.f6]

35. Rxf1 h5 36.Kg1! [At first sight, this position shouldn't be too bad for Black, since the e5–knight's attack on the g6–pawn means that the pawns cannot advance for the moment. However, Kasparov's move makes it all clear; he can afford to take his time, because Black has no constructive moves. The f3–bishop cannot move because of f6 and f7+. The knight must stay on e5 to cover g6, and this ties down the e8–rook too. The rook on d8 cannot achieve anything by itself, since the d-file penetration squares are under control, which leaves only Black's king.]

36...Kf8 37.Bh3 b5 38.Kf2 Kg7?! [Making life easy for White by allowing g4 under favorable circumstances.]

39. g4 Kh6 40.Rg1 hxg4 41.Bxg4 Bxg4 42.Nxg4+ Nxg4+ 43.Rxg4 Rd5 44.f6 Rd1 (44...Rf5+ 45.Kg3a)

45. Ke2 Rg8 46.g7 Kh5 47.Rg2 Rf3 48.Bd4 Kh6 49.c3 Kh5 50.Rg1 Kh6 51.Rg4 Kh5 52.Rxe4 Rf5 53.Re6 Kg6 54.Rxc6 Re8+ 55.Kd2 Rh5 56.Re6 Rh2+ 57.Kd3 Rh3+ 58.Be3 Rd8+ 59.Ke4 Kf7 60.Rc6; b) 45.Ke3! Rf3+ 46.Ke2 Rxc3 47.f7 Rd8 48.g7 Rxc2+ 49.Ke1 Rc1+ 50.Kf2 Rc2+ (50...e3+ 51.Kg2 e2

52. g8Q Rxg8 53.fxg8Q Rg1+ 54.Kf3 Rxg4 55.Qh8+ Kg6 56.Qe8+ Kf5 57.Qf7+ Ke5 58.Kxg4) 51.Kg3 Rc3+ 52.Kh4 Rc1 (52...Rd1 53.g8N+) 53.g8Q Rh1+

54.Kg3 Rg1+ 55.Kf4 Rf1+ 56.Ke5 Rd5+ 57.Ke6 Rf6+ 58.Kxf6 Rd6+; 45...Rf3+ 46.Kh4 Rd8 47.f7 Rd5]

45.g7 [A well-played game by Kasparov, from both the chess and the psychological point of view.] Score: 1–0.

Analysis in terms of computers

The first game shows us many different aspects on how humans differ from machines. We can see how Kasporav created chances from his intuition and opening knowledge that he possessed, whereas the computer just relied on its own intuition and knowledge. The computer just relied on the analysis of 1200000 positions every second, but Kasparov's experience saved him. Experience is very important, due to which he won this game. This reiterates what I said before—humans are extraordinary whereas machines are perfect. Now that we have thoroughly discussed about how chess engines were developed, let's have a look at what has happened to chess engines in the last era. Chess engines can calculate concrete variations but cannot calculate positional chess and have no knowledge whereas humans rely only on knowledge. Due to vast calculations, chess engines could come up with better assessments of certain positions. As we have finished our analysis, we can now go back to how chess has emerged during this decade.

Chess in the last decade

GM RB Ramesh, India's national coach and winner of the 2007 commonwealth championship had an excellent story to tell us how Chess Engines got popular! The impact of chess engines was felt during the end of the 20th century in the 1995 World Championship between Viswanathan Anand and Garry Kasparov. "The first 8 games of this intense world championship match ended in a draw and in the 9th game Anand defeated Kasparov, which was a big shock to the entire world, Kasparov was favorite to win the title and was expected to beat Anand easily, but this did not happen, on the 10th game, Kasparov defeated Anand by using only 5 minutes in his clock!! After the game Kasparov revealed to everyone that they(his team) were using analytical engines to analyze positions, and after this their software was available more readily and they were good in calculation."

After the general public got to know more about it, there was no looking back, the popularity of chess engines soared! Many more grandmasters and amateurs started using chess engines, and today more than a million players use chess engines!! Though the development of Chess Engines have not stopped there! Vidit Gujrati mentioned Project "Leela" (free, open-source, and neural network-based chess engine and distributed computing project. The development has been spearheaded by programmer Gary Linscott, who is also a developer for the Stockfish chess engine.) Alpha Zero and Leela are what I like to call the AI wave in chess! Let's see where Artificial Intelligence takes Chess! Only the future will tell us!

Tips for using a Chess Engine!

This section of the book covers an exclusive interview with GM Pragyananda Rameshbabu and Vidit Gujrati where the young prodigy and India's super grandmaster will give us some insightful tips into how chess players should use chess engines! Don't be surprised to find the same or similar tips in here! Both Grandmasters agree that the best usage of chess engines for chess engines would be advisable for only your openings and your opening preparation! The logic is simple! As GM Vidit is quoted saying "it won't help your calculation!" Though of course just like in any game of chess, there are some expectations to this rule. The advice for using chess engines is simple, though difficult to follow.

AI
&CHESS

Chapter 4

AlphaGo Zero

When we talk about the future, we must talk about AlphaGo Zero owing to its impressive technology. For those of you who do not know what is AlphaGo Zero, imagine this: you teach a small child to play chess, then you ask the little child to go in a small room and ask her to keep playing chess by herself. You then go and see what progress the little child has made. Suddenly, she is better than a world champion. That is exactly what AlphaZero did. It learned chess in four hours just by playing it on its own and beat the best chess engine in the world. Just unbelievable. Time is just a tagline for AlphaGo but the important part is that it just learned by playing it by itself. In this chapter, we will discuss the uniqueness of AlphaGo Zero and what makes it special.

We already know how AlphaZero has made such tremendous contributions to chess with such amazing games and its technology. Now we need to know how AlphaZero works. AlphaZero learns from itself by using a method called reinforcement learning. The software already has a neural network installed in it, which knows nothing about the game expect the rules of the game. The software has a very substantial algorithm. The neural network is designed to work in such a way that it can prognosticate the moves. In each game played by the software, its strength increases, leading to stronger neural networks. Hence, the software would remember its mistakes and get its own type of intuition. It also uses its own neural network to evaluate the current position on the board. I now realize what made Vidit Gujrathi say that it was like "aliens" playing chess. Even the CEO of ChessBase India and IM Sagar Shah said that people thought aliens have come to our world. Mr. Shah also said that he had not seen anything play chess like AlphaZero. In fact, Mr. Shah claimed that even ChessBase was trying to imply similar techniques while developing Komodo 12 which is a chess engine by ChessBase. Mr. Shah also predicted that brute force will soon take a step back and AI will take the stage. Mr. Ramesh also said that chess engines would get more powerful once AI is incorporated, just like we have seen in AlphaGo Zero. Of course many chess players would be concerned if AI could solve chess, which in fact was also one of the main concerns of Mr. Ramesh when he spoke about AI being helpful to chess. I believe that it is highly unlikely that AI will be able to solve chess as humans have been trying it for the last six centuries, and the machines have been trying for only the last century.

As stated earlier, AlphaGo Zero can perform its spectacular feats using the subset of machine learning called reinforcement learning. So let's try to decode how reinforcement learning works and how it has been used in AlphaZero.

Reinforcement learning is when a program or a system can learn from its own mistakes using trial and error through its own exertion and experiences. The goal of the algorithm is to work in the same environment (in this case, chess) and maximize its potential in that environment. To explain this better, let us look at different examples:

- The algorithm could be used in self-driving cars where the environment would be the roads. The algorithm would have a bunch of sensors, which would try to make sense of its surroundings, and by using trial and error, it would maximize its results without causing any other accidents. Hence, test drives on road like situations would be very important before it actually gets on the road.

- Note: In a self-driving car, there will obviously be many other agents and scenarios, but this is just an example

- The algorithm could be a smart thermostat which would get rewards whenever it is close to the temperature target and negative points whenever any individual has to make any changes; hence, through this, it will try to get as accurate as possible.

Policy Search

Policy search is the algorithm which is used by the software agent to determine its actions. An example of a policy would be when a neural network would take in observations as inputs and outputs to take actions. For example, there could be a character from a game who would get a reward for the amount of kills it can get in Fortnite. In this case, the policy for this could be that it has to pick up weapons, try finding other people and start shooting at them. In the case of AlphaZero, the policy is to determine the best chess move at a given position.

How AlphaZero works:

The neural network parameters θ are updated to minimize the error between the predicted outcome vt and the game outcome z, and to maximize the similarity of the policy vector pt to the search probabilities πt. Specifically, the parameters θ are adjusted by gradient descent on a loss function l that sums over mean- squared error and cross-entropy losses,

$$(p, v) = f\theta(s), \qquad l = (z - v) 2 - \pi > \log p + c\|\theta\|2,$$

where c is a parameter controlling the level of L2 weight regularization. The updated parameters are used in subsequent games of self-play.

Gradient descent in the above phrase is an optimization strategy used in machine learning and deep learning to train our model to find the minimum function.

AI
&CHESS

Chapter 5

How does AlphaZero/ Alpha Go Zero work?

Both Alpha Go Zero and Alpha Zero work on similar principles, hence this explanation for this works for both games Chess and Go, hence this explanation would work in both cases.

Alpha Go Zero uses reinforcement learning which uses a policy to decide what action it would take, we could define this policy as **P**, the policy would work as a probability distribution which is the probability of you making the move from any given board position **S**. The value function **V** would then analyse how good the move is, and the algorithm would look at it and go "the probability if I win the game from here".

Alpha Go Zero uses a single Deep Network **F** which is composed of Convoultional layers to estimate P and V.

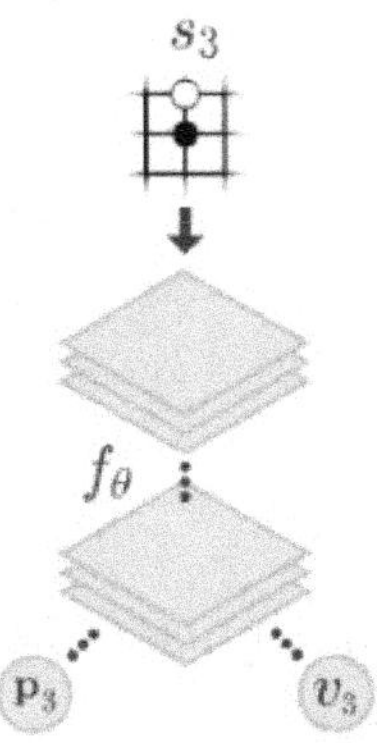

F is trained by playing games against itself, we need to understand how Alpha Zero searches for the next move using Monte Carlo Search Tree.

Monte Carlo Tree Search

In MCTS a search tree is used to *record all sequences* of moves that the program plays, the policy and the value function perform the same task here, but the Monte Carlo search tree aids because it expands the search tree by making a move, hence adding a new position and its previous moves to the search tree. **F** is used to estimate the value of the function and the policy, after which the Action Value function **Q** is used to measure the value of making a move. This is calculated by taking every single move in the set and taking its average. Let's consider an example, in a given position you have 2 choices, Ng5 the probability of winning after ne4 is 0.9 and the probability of winning after ne4 is also 0.9. The Network would then calculate further moves, and take the average probability of all of them to determine the best move. The Q value has a similar purpose to **P** which is estimated by the deep network **P**, the program keeps making more and more moves due to which the search tree keeps growing bigger and bigger, and **Q** gets more accurate.

Key Aspects of How Alpha Zero is self trained:

- Optimization: Using samples in the training data set to optimize F and checkpoint models every 1000 training iterations.

- Evaluator: If the MCTS using the new checkpoint models beats the current best model, we use it as the current best model instead.

- Self-play: Play 25,000 games with the current best model and add them to the training dataset. Only the last 500,000 self-play games are kept for training.

How is the Deep Network (**F**) trained?

F is trained as it starts playing games by itself, the policy(P) and value estimation from the network Monte Carlo Search tree to formulate a more precise policy for the next move. Alpha Go let's MCTS play against itself using different versions of the deep network **F.** After the training is done, the program uses the MCTS with the most optimal network to plan the next move in the real game.

Below you can find a image that will tell you exactly how Alpha Go Zero/ Alpha Go works:

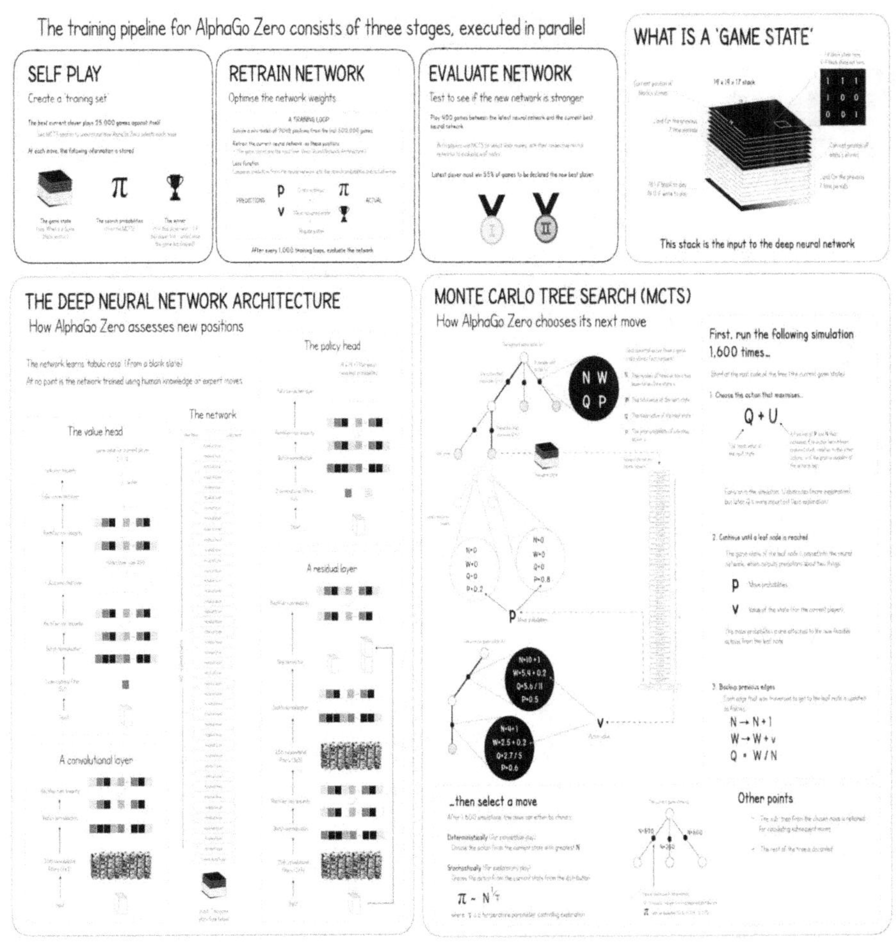

AI
&CHESS

Chapter 6

Future Predictions

In this chapter, I will be predicting AI's impacts on our lives in the coming years.

https://www.pehub.com/vc-journal/five-vcs-predict-future-robotics-ai-rise-surface/ Listed below are some of the predictions:

1. Data is going to be the new oil

Many of you would have surely heard about the recent scandal about Facebook and Cambridge Analytica. Cambridge Analytica is a political consulting firm. The story is full of complex webs. Basically, Facebook let Cambridge Analytica steal data. Data is the information stored of any person. Cambridge Analytica had created a quiz which allowed to them to "steal" data from the users who took this quiz.

This may or may not have affected the election depending on what type of data they had sold. Many news media outlets claim that Cambridge Analytica had affected the election. This could not entirely be true as data collected was not revealed. According to Business Insider, data "could" have been interests, likes, personalities, relationships phots and political affiliation. In its whole article, Business Insider never gives any type of proof or information of how they could have gotten this information. No other media outlets had any confirmed reports of data being stolen on a topic. The only remote confirmation was that the firm had predicted that Trump will win the elections. Hence, I believe that it could have or could have not influenced the election. This entirely depends on the data being stolen. Anyway, Facebook was never aware of what was happening. Being the bigger brand, Facebook had gotten more attention than Cambridge Analytica. So now, you must be wondering why data is so important that it is called as the new oil? How can anyone use it? Now just imagine if Cambridge

Analytica had gotten data about a person or a group of friends that did not like gun control rules in America. They further investigate into this matter and find out that not only the group of friends but the people living in that city do not like the rules of gun control in the United States. This information is now delivered to Trump. Trump decides that he will give a speech for gun control in that city so that the people would like him and give him their votes, but Trump never really thinks of implementing that rule. This is just an example of how stealing data could influence a certain thing. This could sometimes be good but imagine if they sell this data to an unworthy third party. There is also a special term for the incidents described above—data mining. This data, if not sold, could also be used in making machines, just like AlphaZero from different machines with different data and a different purpose. Just like data is going to be the new oil, it is going to be a much more effective oil. Data could be infinite whereas oil is finite. It surely could be a fast-growing industry which could have many potential investors and many benefits. There are also some disadvantages. In this digital world, data could surely be the new oil, but this oil was already mined very long ago by the tech titans like Alphabet, Facebook, Amazon and Microsoft; they have a very big head start which could be a big threat to everyone. Data is now available in large quantities. Almost all activities today need data; while going from one place to another, people use Google Maps, thereby creating more and more digital traces for each person. Tech giants, with the help of their algorithms, could predict what a customer is going to buy, where he is going to go and many other predictions. With this, they could help improve their experience of their searches, which would attract more users. This means that soon, these companies could generate and create revenues or could also be threating if these files somehow got hacked, which is highly unlikely. Hence, there would be many benefits and many disadvantages regarding data.

2. Self-driving cars

All of us must have heard a lot about self-driving cars and Elon Musk. According to National Highway Traffic Safety, 94% of the car crashes occur because of human error. So technically, it makes a lot of sense to use self-driving cars to prevent accidents. There are many pros and cons while discussing handing over our driving to technology. The idea behind self-driving cars is just to prevent these accidents from happening. Their aim is to navigate their way through obstacles, obey traffic laws in the country they are in and make them reach safely to their destination. The basic idea of this is also done by detecting obstacles using built in cameras, radars, solar, GPS and the infrared sensor processor. Below are images of the sensor which are used. A car can also communicate with other cars to reduce traffic and congestion.

https://www.businessinsider.sg/how-driverless-cars-might-change-cities-2016-12/?r=US&IR=T The above image shows the built-in camera.

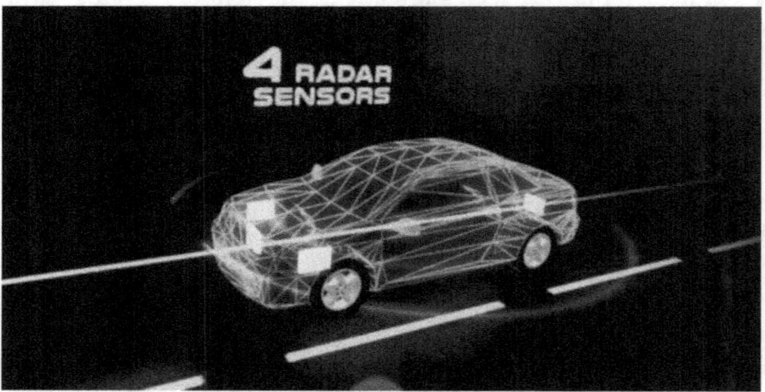

https://thenextweb.com/cars/2017/03/31/radar-system-envisions-safer-future-self-driving-cars/ The above image shows the radar sensors and how they work.

Some self-driving cars could be powered with solar panels; the image below is a car with a solar panel.

https://auto.howstuffworks.com/fuel-efficiency/vehicles/solar-powered-vehicle-possibility2.htm Finally, below we have an image of how everything works together.

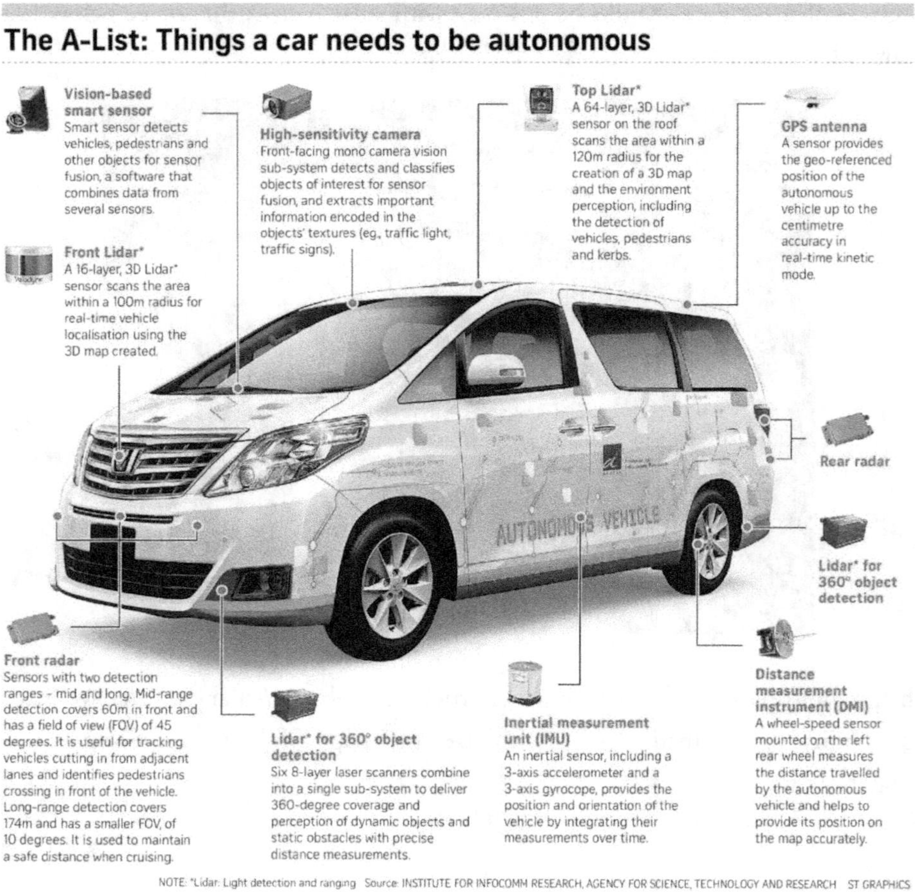

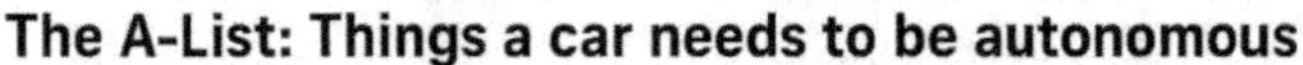

The A-List: Things a car needs to be autonomous

Vision-based smart sensor
Smart sensor detects vehicles, pedestrians and other objects for sensor fusion, a software that combines data from several sensors.

Front Lidar*
A 16-layer, 3D Lidar* sensor scans the area within a 100m radius for real-time vehicle localisation using the 3D map created.

High-sensitivity camera
Front-facing mono camera vision sub-system detects and classifies objects of interest for sensor fusion, and extracts important information encoded in the objects' textures (eg., traffic light, traffic signs).

Top Lidar*
A 64-layer, 3D Lidar* sensor on the roof scans the area within a 120m radius for the creation of a 3D map and the environment perception, including the detection of vehicles, pedestrians and kerbs.

GPS antenna
A sensor provides the geo-referenced position of the autonomous vehicle up to the centimetre accuracy in real-time kinetic mode.

Rear radar

Lidar* for 360° object detection

Front radar
Sensors with two detection ranges – mid and long. Mid-range detection covers 60m in front and has a field of view (FOV) of 45 degrees. It is useful for tracking vehicles cutting in from adjacent lanes and identifies pedestrians crossing in front of the vehicle. Long-range detection covers 174m and has a smaller FOV, of 10 degrees. It is used to maintain a safe distance when cruising.

Lidar* for 360° object detection
Six 8-layer laser scanners combine into a single sub-system to deliver 360-degree coverage and perception of dynamic objects and static obstacles with precise distance measurements.

Inertial measurement unit (IMU)
An inertial sensor, including a 3-axis accelerometer and a 3-axis gyrocope, provides the position and orientation of the vehicle by integrating their measurements over time.

Distance measurement instrument (DMI)
A wheel-speed sensor mounted on the left rear wheel measures the distance travelled by the autonomous vehicle and helps to provide its position on the map accurately.

NOTE: *Lidar: Light detection and ranging   Source: INSTITUTE FOR INFOCOMM RESEARCH, AGENCY FOR SCIENCE, TECHNOLOGY AND RESEARCH   ST GRAPHICS

https://www.straitstimes.com/singapore/transport/concept-of-self-driving-vehicles-gains-pace

Now, the question remains: Is this technology good or bad? Below is a table which talks about all the pros and cons of self-driving cars.

94% of the accidents are caused by human mistakes. Self-driving cars use a lot of complex algorithms as shown in the figure above. Hence, many taxi drivers will lose their jobs, and as they are not specialized, they will not be able to get another job. The chances of an accident are dramatically reduced.

Many jobs from the car insurance companies could also be lost, as a thing like car insurance would become extinct. A computer cannot be distracted. How many times have you seen an adult talking on a phone while driving a car? According to auto insurance data, this is the leading cause of accidents in the United States.

A taxi driver would need to re-train as driving a self-driving car would need knowledge on the driver's part as well. These drivers should be specialized as there could be many IT equipment they would have to deal with. Travelling time could be saved. While your machine is driving your car, you can always talk on the phone or make your social life better.

The new technology would be very expensive as the cost of the sensors would already be more than hundred thousand American dollars. Disabled individuals could easily travel on these cars.

As shown in the movie Fast and Furious 8, self-driving cars could be hacked. As self-driving cars can communicate with themselves, they can save travelling time. Self-driving cars, just like the tech giants, could store a lot of personal data. A traffic police could be now doing more serious work such as working on some very interesting crimes which could make a novel.

In case of a highly unlikely car accident, we will never know who is liable—is it the car manufacturer, the driver or the software developer?

As we can see in the above list, there are many pros and cons on self-driving cars. It is hard to know if this technology is good or bad. I believe that self-driving cars are going to be very beneficial to everyone and would surely increase everyone's safety. Just like the Industrial Revolution where many people lost their jobs and had many various disadvantages, after about three decades, we saw that it was for the greater good. Just like this, the AI revolution is also just a transition which is meant for the greater good.

AI
& CHESS

Conclusion

We have covered how AI will revolutionize the world in which we live—from sports to cars and everything. AI will surely take many jobs away but also give many jobs. Only time can tell what the future has in store for us.

AI
&CHESS

Special Acknowledgments

GM Vidit Gujrathi
FIDE Elo: 2715
Title: Grandmaster

It was a great opportunity to meet Vidit Gujrathi who was a very humble and down-to-earth guy. It was a great honor to meet and take his interview for my book. I hope we can see him as the next world champion soon. It is a great honor to be just writing my name next to his.

GM Praggnanandhaa Rameshbabu
FIDE Elo: 2532
Title: Grandmaster

Praggnanandhaa Rameshbabu is a chess prodigy from India who is the second youngest person to achieve the title of GM and the youngest in the world. Praggnananandhaa had just achieved his grandmaster title when we had met in Pardubice open where I had a chance to take his interview. Praggnanandhaa was very friendly and down to earth. He had no sense of superiority and just wanted to continue playing chess. It was a great pleasure to meet him.

GM Ramesh RB FIDE Elo: 2472
Title: Grandmaster

An ocean of vast knowledge was the first impression I got when I met him. While meeting Mr Ramesh in one of his chess camps in Mumbai, I had the amazing opportunity to learn many new ideas, and I was also able to improve my calculations. Luckily, I was also able to take an interview with him for my book. Mr Ramesh was a great guy, down-to-earth, intelligent and a great chess coach. His contributions to the country are also remarkable. His coaching has brought grandmasters like Pragyandha, Arvind Chithambaram and many other youngsters. He himself, as a player, has also won the British Chess Championships and the Commonwealth Chess Championships in 2007. While interviewing him, it is hard not to think that his knowledge is vast and has no boundaries.

IM Sagar Shah
FIDE Elo: 2407
Title: International Master CEO of ChessBase India

A very amazing all-rounder. He is a chartered accountant, the CEO of ChessBase India and a chess player. During his interview, he had given me a lot of information about how we use chess engines. Unfortunately, I was only able to meet him for a short time as I was playing in the Mumbai Mayor's Cup during that time. He himself has interviewed so many people being a CEO of such a big firm. He has also written many articles.

IM Chandrashekhar Gokhale
FIDE Elo: 2189
Title: International Master

Chandrashekhar Gokhale is another all-rounder who is soon to be a doctor. He is a chess player, a chess coach, a chess dad, and works in Air India. Mr. Gokhale, my beloved chess coach, really helped me in my whole journey of writing this book and my chess career. I have known him for quite some time, and he has also helped me in various obstacles throughout my life. During his interview, most of his opinions were old school, and he had also given me very nice ideas.

AI
&CHESS

Appendix

As promised, in the appendix, I have provided a few games played between Alpha Go Zero and Stockfish, these crazy games must be checked on the board! I have entered a few variations, from a few games but under no circumstances, I have analysed these games. The games are very complicated and something of a superhuman characteristic.

Alpha Go Zero Vs Stockfish Game 1

Would you rather be a peice up or have an extra piece that's useless?

1. d4 e6 2. e4 d5 3. Nc3 Nf6 4. e5 Nfd7 5. f4 c5 6. Nf3 cxd4 7. Nb5 Bb4+ 8. Bd2 Bc5 9. b4 Be7 10. Nbxd4 Nc6 11. c3 a5 12. b5 Nxd4 13. cxd4 Nb6 14. a4 Nc4 15. Bd3 Nxd2 16. Kxd2 Bd7 17. Ke3 b6 18. g4 h5 19. Qg1 hxg4 20. Qxg4 Bf8 21. h4 Qe7 22. Rhc1 g6 23. Rc2 Kd8 24. Racl Qe8 25. Rc7 Rc8 26. Rxc8+ Bxc8 27. Rc6 Bb7 28. Rc2 Kd7 29. Ng5 Be7 30. Bxg6 Bxg5 31. Qxg5 fxg6 32. f5 Rg8 33. Qh6 Qf7 34. f6 Kd8 35. Kd2 Kd7 36. Rc1 Kd8 37. Qe3 Qf8 38. Qc3 Qb4 39. Qxb4 axb4 40. Rg1 b3 41. Kc3 Bc8 42. Kxb3 Bd7 43. Kb4 Be8 44. Ra1 Kc7 45. a5 Bd7 46. axb6+ Kxb6 47. Ra6+ Kb7 48. Kc5 Rd8 49. Ra2 Rc8+ 50. Kd6 Be8 51. Ke7 g5 52. hxg5 1-0.

Alpha Go Zero Vs StockFish Game 2

1. Nf3 Nf6 2. c4 b6 3. d4 e6 4. g3 Ba6 5. Qc2 c5 6. d5 exd5 7. cxd5 Bb7 (7... Nxd5 8. Qe4+) 8. Bg2 Nxd5 9. O-O Nc6 10. Rd1 Be7 11. Qf5 (11. Rxd5 Nb4) 11... Nf6 12. e4 g6 13. Qf4 O-O 14. e5 Nh5 15. Qg4 Re8 16. Nc3 (16. Rxd7 Qc8 17. Nc3 Bf6 {Slightly better for black, he will get the pawn back and the pin is very annoying} 18. exf6 15 Nxf6) 16... Qb8 17. Nd5 Bf8 18. Bf4 Qc8 19. h3

Ne7 20. Ne3 Bc6 21. Rd6 Ng7 22. Rf6 Qb7 23. Bh6 Nd5 24. Nxd5 Bxd5 25. Rd1 Ne6 26. Bxf8 Rxf8 27. Qh4 Bc6 28. Qh6 Rae8 29. Rd6 Bxf3 30. Bxf3 Qa6 31. h4 Qa5 32. Rd1 c4 33. Rd5 Qe1+ 34. Kg2 c3 35. bxc3 Qxc3 36. h5 Re7 37. Bd1 Qe1 38. Bb3 Rd8 39. Rf3 Qe4 40. Qd2 Qg4 41. Bd1 Qe4 42. h6 Nc7 43. Rd6 Ne6 44. Bb3 Qxe5 45. Rd5 Qh8 46. Qb4 Nc5 47. Rxc5 bxc5 48. Qh4 Rde8 49. Rf6 Rf8 50. Qf4 a5 51. g4 d5 52. Bxd5 Rd7 53. Bc4 a4 54. g5 a3 55. Qf3 Rc7 56. Qxa3 Qxf6 57. gxf6 Rfc8 58. Qd3 Rf8 59. Qd6 Rfc8 60. a4 1-0.

Alpha Go Zero Vs StockFish Game 3

1. d4 Nf6 2. Nf3 e6 3. c4 b6 4. g3 Be7 5. Bg2 Bb7 6. O-O O-O 7. d5 exd5 8. Nh4 c6 9. cxd5 Nxd5 {Alpha Go Zero loves giving up pawns.} 10. Nf5 Nc7 11. e4 Bf6 12. Nd6 Ba6 13. Re1 Ne8 14. e5 Nxd6 15. exf6 Qxf6 {One more pawn given!} 16. Nc3 Bc4 17. h4 h6 18. b3 Qxc3 19. Bf4 Nb7 20. bxc4 Qf6 21. Be4 Na6 22. Be5 Qe6 23. Bd3 f6 24. Bd4 Qf7 25. Qg4 Rfd8 26. Re3 Nac5 27. Bg6 Qf8 28. Rd1 Rab8 29. Kg2 Ne6 30. Bc3 Nbc5 31. Rde1 Na4 32. Bd2 Kh8 33. f4 Qd6 34. Bc1 Nd4 35. Re7 f5 36. Bxf5 Nxf5 37. Qxf5 Rf8 38. Rxd7 Rxf5 39. Rxd6 Rf7 40. g4 Kg8 41. g5 hxg5 42. hxg5 Nc5 43. Kf3 Nb7 44. Rdd1 (44. Rxc6 Na5 45. Rd6 Nxc4) 44... Na5 45. Re4 c5 46. Bb2 Nc6 47. g6 Rc7 48. Kg4 Nd4 49. Rd2 Rf8 50. Bxd4 cxd4 51. Rdxd4 Rfc8 52. Kg5 Rf8 53. Rd2 Rc6 54. Rd5 Rc7 55. f5 Rb7 56. a3 Rc7 57. a4 a6 58. Red4 Rcc8 59. Re5 Rc7 60. a5 Rc5 61. Rxc5 bxc5 62. Rd6 Ra8 63. Re6 Kf8 64. Rc6 Ke7 65. Kf4 Kd7 66. Rxc5 Rh8 67. Rd5+ Ke7 68. Re5+ Kd7 69. Re6 Rh4+ 70. Kg5 *

These games would have surely blown your minds away! The way Alpha Zero beats Stockfish is how a Grandmaster would beat a amatuer who probably tried playing at his best. Looking at the way Alpha plays, we all could tell that it has a very aggressive style of play, squeezing the heck out of his opponent! We could also see that in every game Alpha Zero started, Alpha Zero loved putting the opponent's pieces in awkward places even if that meant sacrificing a pawn or 2. We could clearly see this in games 1 and 2, soon after which Alpha Zero would press and sooner or later it would win the game!

Bibiliography

Duckett, Chris. "DeepMind AlphaGo Zero Learns on Its Own without Meatbag Intervention." *ZDNet*, ZDNet, 19 Oct. 2017, www.zdnet.com/article/deepmind-alphago-zero-learns-on-its-own-without-meatbag-intervention.

Foster, David. "AlphaGo Zero Explained In One Diagram." *Medium*, Applied Data Science, 2 Dec. 2019, medium.com/applied-data-science/alphago-zero-explained-in-one-diagram-365f5abf67e0.

Hui, Jonathan. "AlphaGo Zero - a Game Changer. (How It Works?)." *Medium*, Medium, 13 Oct. 2018, medium.com/@jonathan_hui/alphago-zero-a-game-changer-14ef6e45eba5.

Hui, Jonathan. "Monte Carlo Tree Search (MCTS) in AlphaGo Zero." *Medium*, Medium, 20 May 2018, medium.com/@jonathan_hui/monte-carlo-tree-search-mcts-in-alphago-zero-8a403588276a.

Knapton, Sarah. "AlphaGo Zero: Google DeepMind Supercomputer Learns 3,000 Years of Human Knowledge in 40 Days." *The Telegraph*, Telegraph Media Group, 18 Oct. 2017, www.telegraph.co.uk/science/2017/10/18/alphago-zero-google-deepmind-supercomputer-learns-3000-years.

Watson, Sarah Knapton; Leon. "Entire Human Chess Knowledge Learned and Surpassed by DeepMind's AlphaZero in Four Hours." *The Telegraph*, Telegraph Media Group, 6 Dec. 2017, www.telegraph.co.uk/science/2017/12/06/entire-human-chess-knowledge-learned-surpassed-deepminds-alphazero.

Works Cited

1. Artificial Intelligence. Techopedia.com, Copyright © 2018 Techopedia Inc., 2018, www.techopedia.com/definition/190/artificial-intelligence-ai.

2. Boslet, Mark. "As Five VCs Predict the Future, Robotics and AI Rise to the Surface." PE Hub, VCJ, 24 May 2018, www.pehub.com/vc-journal/five-vcs-predict-future-robotics-ai-rise-surface/.

3. Brain, Marshall. "How Chess Computers Work." HowStuffWorks, 1 Apr. 2000, electronics.howstuffworks.com/chess1.htm.

4. Chandler_1. "Computers and Chess." How Do Chess Engines Work?, Chess.com, 10 Feb. 2014, www.chess.com/blog/Chandler_1/how-do-chess-engines-work.

5. Collados, Jose Camacho. "Is AlphaZero Really a Scientific Breakthrough in AI?" Medium, Augmenting Humanity, 11 Dec. 2017, medium.com/@josecamachocollados/is-alphazero-really-a-   scientific-breakthrough-in-ai-bf66ae1c84f2.

6. Data. "286." Data, Cambridge Dictionary, 2018, dictionary.cambridge.org/dictionary/english/data.

7. Grabianowski, Ed. "How Speech Recognition Works." HowStuffWorks, 10 Nov. 2006, electronics.howstuffworks.com/gadgets/high-tech-gadgets/speech-recognition1.htm.

8. Hitesh, Bhagat Raj, and Karan Bajaj. "All You Need to Know about Voice Recognition." The Economic Times, 17 Oct. 2011, economictimes.indiatimes.com/tech/software/all-you-need-to-know-   about-voice-recognition/articleshow/10383593.cms.

9. Krishna, Arvind. "AI Learns the Art of Debate with IBM Project Debater." IBM Cognitive Advantage Reports, IBM Corporation, 19 June 2018, www.ibm.com/blogs/research/2018/06/ai-debate/.

10. Larson, Erik J. "A Brief History of Computer Chess." The Best Schools, 2018, thebestschools.org/magazine/brief-history-of-computer-chess/.

11. Marr, Bernard. "A Short History of Machine Learning -- Every Manager Should Read." Forbes, Forbes Magazine, 8 Mar. 2016, www.forbes.com/sites/bernardmarr/2016/02/19/a-short-history-of- machine-learning-every-manager-should-read/.

12. Saltzman, Marc. "Are We Close to a Future of Self-Driving Cars?" AARP, Sitemap, 7 Feb. 2018, www.aarp.org/auto/trends-lifestyle/info-2018/future-driverless-cars-fd.html.

13. Srivastava, Sanjay. "Defining AI: Reasoning, Interaction and Learning." CIO, CIO, 9 Nov. 2017, www.cio.com/article/3236784/artificial-intelligence/defining-ai-reasoning-interaction-and-learning.html.

14. The world's most valuable resource is no longer oil, but data. The Economist, 6 May 2017, www.economist.com/leaders/2017/05/06/the-worlds-most-valuable-resource-is-no-longer-oil-but-data.

15. Top 20 Pros and Cons Associated with Self-Driving Cars. Cheap Auto Insurance Quotes, AutoInsurance, 2018, www.autoinsurancecenter.com/top-20-pros-and-cons-associated-with-self-driving- cars.htm.

16. Weiss, Brennan. "Trump-Linked Firm Cambridge Analytica Collected Personal Information from 50 Million Facebook Users without Permission." Business Insider, 17 Mar. 2018, www.businessinsider.com/cambridge-analytica-trump-firm-facebook-data-50-million-users-2018-3/.

17. "What Are Heuristics?" WeLiveSecurity, 29 Dec. 2010, www.welivesecurity.com/2010/12/29/what-are-heuristics/.

18. What is Artificial Intelligence. "What Is Artificial Intelligence (AI)? - Definition from Techopedia." Techopedia.com, Copyright © 2018 Techopedia Inc., 2018, www.techopedia.com/definition/190/artificial-intelligence-ai.

19. What is Machine Learning. Expert System, Expert System, 5 Oct. 2017, www.expertsystem.com/machine-learning-definition/.